Adelina Aviator

Story by Jessica Vana

Illustrations by Adam Dix

To all the missionary kids who've left people and places they love to tell the greatest Story of all. Thank you.

And to Phil, for making this adventure so much fun. Je t'aime.

J.V.

For Sophie

A.D.

Published in the United States by Credo House Publishers,
a division of Credo Communications, LLC, Grand Rapids, Michigan
www.credohousepublishers.com

ISBN-13: 978-1-625860-02-6

Cover layout and interior design:
Sharon VanLoozenoord

Once upon a time (but not that long ago) two aviators fell in love.

They got married and had a
daughter they called "Adelina Aviator."

Adelina loved words and she loved airplanes.
In fact, one of her very first words was "Airplane!"

When Adelina was little, her daddy went to school to learn to fix airplanes. Adelina loved helping in the shop. She was always eager to help find the right tool or troubleshoot a sputtering engine. “Oh, I can fix *that*!” she'd tell her dad.

“Adelina Aviator, you are such a big helper!” the mechanics would say. “We've never met a little girl who loves airplanes as much as you!”

By her third birthday, Adelina knew all about engines and propellers. She even knew fancy airplane words like *fuselage* and *aileron*. Adelina would tell her friends all about what she learned in the airplane hangar, and they'd laugh together as she taught them how to yell "Clear prop!" before starting an engine.

Every night at bedtime Adelina's momma would kiss her cheek three times and whisper, "Bonne nuit. Je t'aime, ma petite bébé.* God bless you and give you courage, my little missionary aviator."

*Good night. I love you, my little baby.

"Momma, what's courage?" Adelina asked one night. Momma looked long into Adelina's brown eyes and smiled. "Courage is when God asks you to do something big, bigger than you ever thought you could do, and you do it."

One cozy afternoon, Adelina discovered that she and her family would be moving to the jungle to fly airplanes. They would use the airplanes to bring hope and good news to people.

“How can we use airplanes to help people?” Adelina asked.

“We can use our airplane to bring people the things they need,” Dad smiled. “Things like Bibles, food, and medicine. Best of all, we will get to tell our new friends in the jungle all about God’s great love!”

Adelina went to bed that night thinking about what life would be like in the jungle.

In the morning Adelina had some questions.

Adelina was excited to start packing for the jungle but began thinking about how different life would be without her friends, most of her toys, and especially . . . her grandma.

At bedtime, Adelina was uneasy. “Momma, moving to the jungle will be hard, huh? I hope I can find my courage.”

Softly and slowly Momma tucked Aviator Bear under Adelina’s arm. “When you feel like this adventure is too big, hold on to Aviator Bear and remember: God can give you courage as big as the night sky.” Momma looked out the window and nodded. Wink. Kiss-kiss-kiss. Lights out.

Before their adventure began, Adelina and her family had to get a little more training.

When Adelina got to Missionary Aviator Training Camp, she met all kinds of super cool kids.

Holding Aviator Bear extra tight, Adelina told her new friends, "I'm happy to move to the jungle, but I sure am going to miss my grandma!"

"Yeah," said Allan Aviator. "I'm going to miss my best friend Brady. And my trampoline!"

"And I'm going to miss my bedroom," sighed Annie Aviator.

On a misty Tuesday morning, Adelina had one last thing to do before her big trip to the jungle. She had to say goodbye to her grandparents.

At the airport Adelina's Grandma Helena gave her a fancy aviator quilt, and her Grandpa Jay gave her a pack of his favorite gum (to help her ears pop on the airplane).

When Adelina reached out to hug her, Grandma Helena's eyes drip-dropped giant, soppy tears.

"Oh! Adelina Aviator, I love you so. I don't know how to let you go. I love you very big!" she said, making a lemony face.

Adelina felt a great big sad feeling in her tummy, and she thought for a moment. She thought about how much she loved her grandparents, her bedroom, her backyard, her doggy, and her friends. Then she remembered her momma's words about courage and asked God to help her be brave. Suddenly, a silly, happy thought popped into her head.

"Grandma, there are kids in the jungle who don't have a Bible yet! Can you believe that? They don't know about Jesus, and I have to go tell them! They're waiting for me, Grandma! Here! *You* keep Aviator Bear, and when you snuggle him remember that God can give you courage as big as the night sky!" With each word she said, Adelina Aviator felt braver and braver.

Adelina Aviator scrunched her little nose and, with a quick sniffle, took those last steps toward her new life. Suddenly, she felt a brand new feeling. It was the feeling of true courage, and she knew . . . she had *work* to do.

Be strong and courageous. Do not be terrified; do not be discouraged, for the LORD *your God will be with you wherever you go.* JOSHUA 1:9